First Facts

Whales and Dolphins Up Close

BLUE WHALES UP CLOSE

by Jody Sullivan Rake

Consultant:
Deborah Nuzzolo
Education Manager
SeaWorld, San Diego

Capstone press

Mankato, Minnesota

First Facts is published by Capstone Press,
151 Good Counsel Drive, P.O. Box 669, Mankato, Minnesota 56002.
www.capstonepress.com

Library of Congress Cataloging-in-Publication Data
Rake, Jody Sullivan.
    Blue whales up close / by Jody Sullivan Rake.
    p. cm. — (First facts. Whales and dolphins up close)
    Includes bibliographical references and index.
    Summary: "Presents an up-close look at blue whales, including their body features,
habitat, and life cycle" — Provided by publisher.
    ISBN 978-1-4296-3336-9 (library binding)
    1. Blue whale — Juvenile literature. I. Title. II. Series.
QL737.C424R35 2010
599.5'248 — dc22   2009006005

Editorial Credits
Megan Schoeneberger, editor; Renée T. Doyle, set designer; Alison Thiele, book
    designer; Wanda Winch, media researcher

Photo Credits
Ardea/Francois Gohier, cover, 18
Minden Pictures/Flip Nicklin, 13 (right), 21
Nature Picture Library/Doc White, 9
SeaPics.com/Doc White, 7 (both), 10; Mike Johnson, 12–13; Phillip Colla, 1, 4–5, 15,
    17, 20
Shutterstock/Marilyn Volan, 2–3, 19, 24
www.marinethemes.com/Mark Conlin, 8

TABLE OF CONTENTS

Bigger Than Dinosaurs

Blue whales are the biggest animals on earth. These ocean **mammals** are larger than the largest dinosaurs.

mammal — a warm-blooded animal that has a backbone

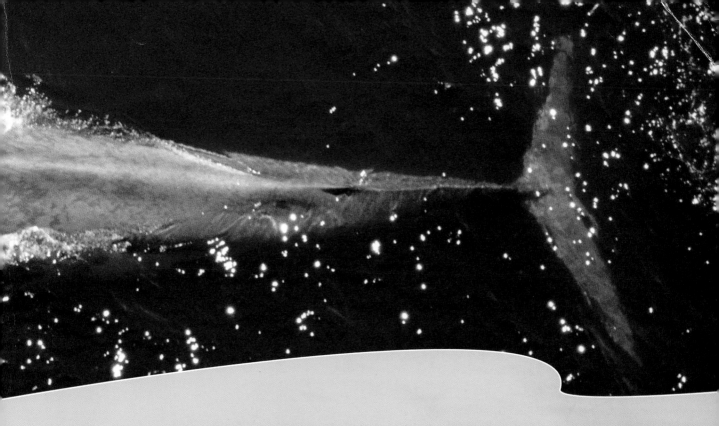

Blue whales grow up to 90 feet (27 meters) long. That's almost as long as three school buses. They weigh at least 220,000 pounds (99,800 kilograms), which is more than 15 large elephants.

No Teeth

Blue whales use **baleen** to strain food from the water. Instead of teeth, up to 400 baleen plates hang down from their upper jaws. Baleen is stiff. It has hairy edges near the whale's tongue. Baleen can be 40 inches (102 centimeters) long at the back of the mouth.

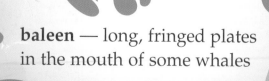

baleen — long, fringed plates in the mouth of some whales

baleen

A Whale's Mustache

Baleen is made of **keratin**.
Keratin is the same stuff that makes
up fingernails and hair in people.
Baleen looks like a mustache inside
the whale's mouth.

keratin — the hard substance that
forms hair, fingernails, or baleen

7

Huge Hunger, Tiny Prey

What does the largest creature in the world eat? Some of the littlest food, that's what! Blue whales dine on small shrimplike animals called krill. Krill travel in huge pink swarms throughout the sea. The colder the water, the more krill whales find.

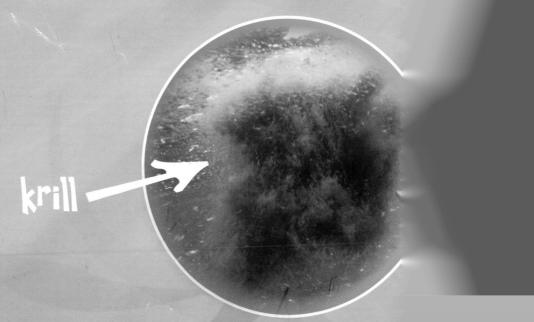

krill

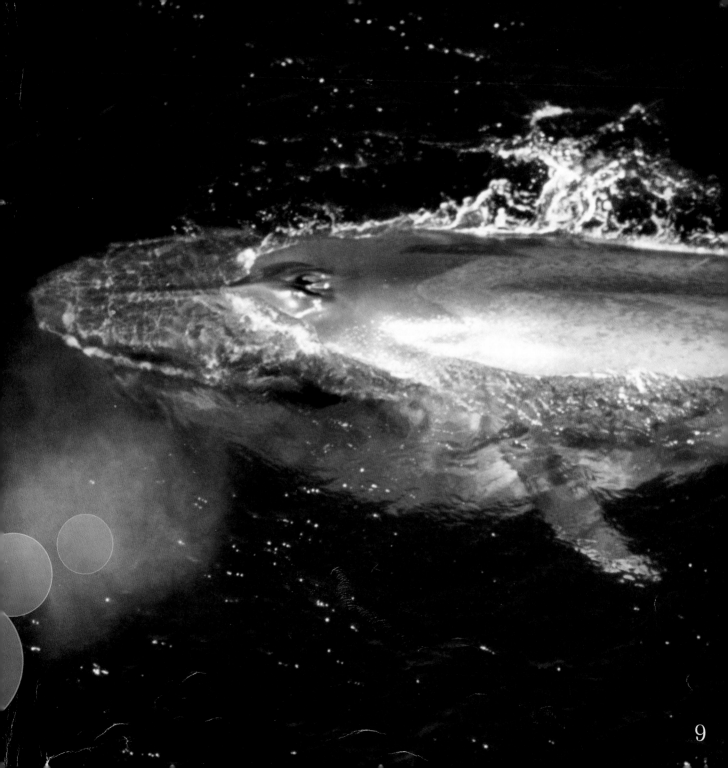

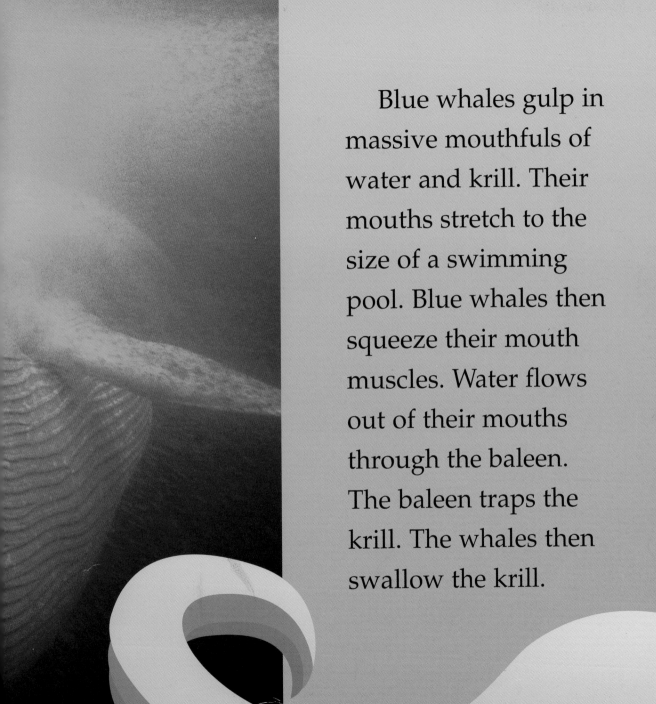

Blue whales gulp in massive mouthfuls of water and krill. Their mouths stretch to the size of a swimming pool. Blue whales then squeeze their mouth muscles. Water flows out of their mouths through the baleen. The baleen traps the krill. The whales then swallow the krill.

Blowholes and Flippers

Blue whales breathe air through two blowholes. A small ridge in front of the blowholes steers water away when breathing.

A blue whale's smooth skin is grayish blue with light blue spots. Its short flippers come to a point. A tiny dorsal fin rests near its tail. Powerful tail flukes push the whale through the water.

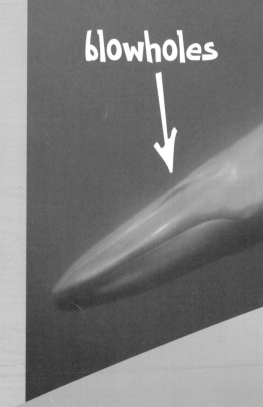

blowholes

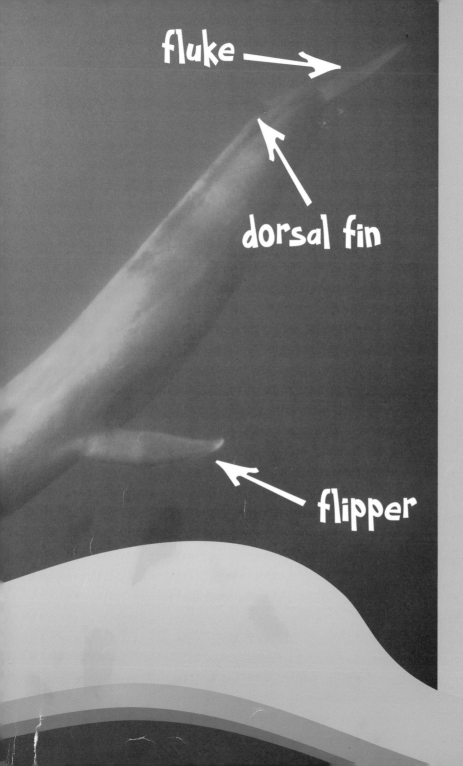

fluke →

dorsal fin

flipper

A Blue Whale's Blow

When a whale breathes out, air and water droplets shoot up into the air. The spray is called blow. A blue whale's blow is tall and straight. It can be up to 30 feet (9 meters) tall. That's as tall as a three-story building!

Life in the Sea

Blue whales live in all the world's oceans. In winter, blue whales migrate to warmer water near the equator.

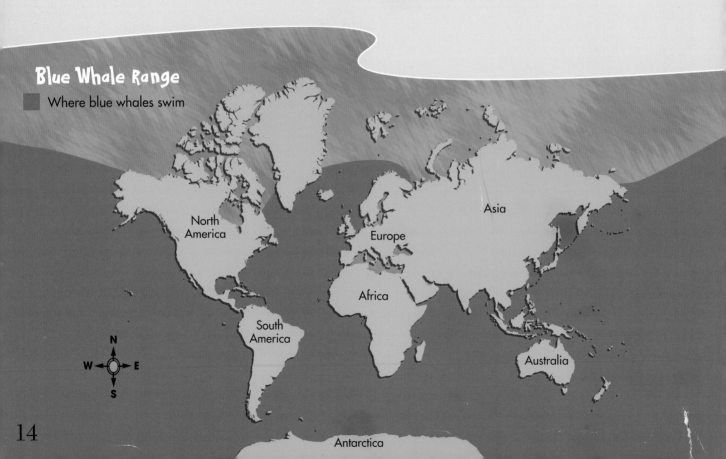

Blue Whale Range

Where blue whales swim

North America

South America

Europe

Africa

Asia

Australia

Antarctica

N
W E
S

Blue whales are usually seen alone
or in pairs. During summer, blue
whales often feed together.

Life Cycle

Blue whales are old enough to mate when they are 6 to 10 years old. Male and female whales mate during winter in warm tropical waters. One year later, females give birth. A female may have a calf every two or three years.

Life Cycle of a Blue Whale

Calf

Blue whale calves weigh up to 6,000 pounds (2,722 kilograms).

Mom and Baby

Young

Young whales drink their mother's milk until they are about 8 months old.

Adult

Blue whales can live to be 70 years old.

Baby Blues

Blue whale calves are bigger than most other adult whales. They are up to 27 feet (8 meters) long. Calves gulp 100 gallons (379 liters) of their mother's milk each day. In less than a year, calves grow to almost eight times their birth weight.

Amazing but True!

Blue whales make low, deep rumbling noises. Other blue whales can hear these noises more than 100 miles (161 kilometers) away. The sounds are so low that you probably could not hear them. But you could feel them, just like you can feel a stereo speaker vibrating.

Blue Whales and People

In the early 1900s, whalers hunted thousands of whales. Blue whales were hunted most often. Before whaling, about 350,000 blue whales roamed the seas. Whalers killed almost all of them. Laws now protect the whales. Their population is slowly growing, but they are still endangered.

Glossary

baleen (BAY-leen) — long, fringed plates in the mouths of some whales

dorsal fin (DOR-suhl FIN) — the fin that sticks up from a whale's back

fluke (FLOOK) — the wide, flat area at the end of a whale's tail; whales move their flukes to swim.

keratin (KAIR-uh-tin) — the hard substance that forms hair, fingernails, or baleen

krill (KRIL) — small, shrimplike animals

mammal (MAM-uhl) — a warm–blooded animal that breathes air; mammals have hair or fur; female mammals feed milk to their young.

migrate (MYE-grate) — to move from one place to another

whaling (WAYL-ing) — hunting whales for their meat, oil, and bones

Read More

Nicklin, Flip, and Linda Nicklin. *Face to Face with Whales.* Face to Face with Animals. Washington, D.C.: National Geographic, 2008.

Smith, Molly. *Blue Whale: The World's Biggest Mammal.* SuperSized! New York: Bearport, 2007.

Spilsbury, Louise, and Richard Spilsbury. *Blue Whale.* Save Our Animals! Chicago: Heinemann, 2006.

Internet Sites

FactHound offers a safe, fun way to find Internet sites related to this book. All of the sites on FactHound have been researched by our staff.

Here's all you do:

Visit *www.facthound.com*

FactHound will fetch the best sites for you!

Index